TREVOR WYE

PRACTICE BOOK
for the

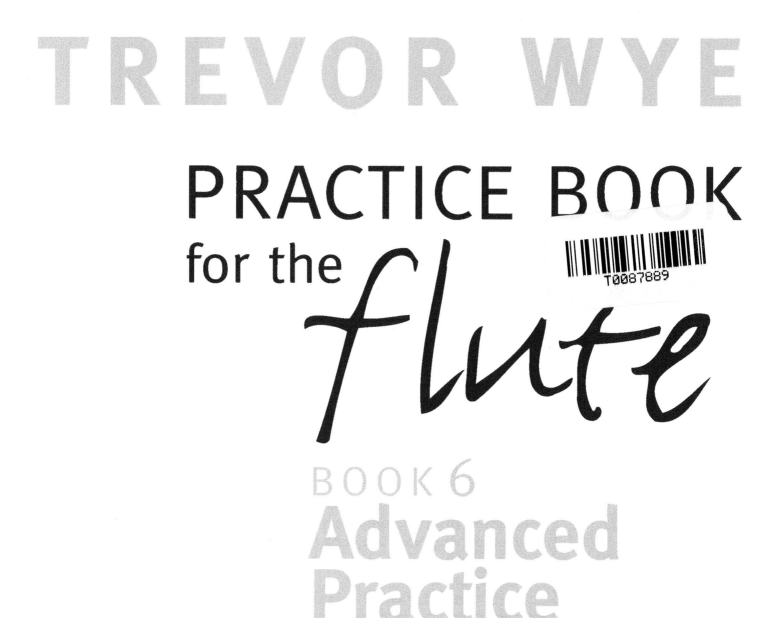

flute

BOOK 6
Advanced
Practice

NOVELLO

DISTRIBUTED BY

HAL•LEONARD®
CORPORATION
7777 W. BLUEMOUND RD. P.O. BOX 13819 MILWAUKEE, WI 53213

For GEOFFREY GILBERT with affection

CONTENTS

FOREWORD

This is the final book for the flute in this series. Much of it is a continuation of the exercises set out in the earlier books; some of it breaks new ground. Most of it is for advanced players; some of it for beginner and advanced player alike. Take what you, or your students, need. More detailed information and explanation will be found in *Proper Flute Playing* – Trevor Wye (Novello) 1987, a companion book to the entire Practice Book series.

A PREFACE TO BE READ

TO THE STUDENT

This book is about practising; how to extract the most from it, how to be more efficient at it and how to isolate and overcome some of the difficulties of the flute. It is by no means intended to be definitive. It was written to help you achieve good results with many of the flute problems, in the shortest time.

If the exercises are practised properly, it will shorten the time spent on the building blocks of flute playing, and so allow more time for music making.

These points about practising in general, are important:

(a) Practise the flute only because you *want* to; if you don't want to – don't! It is almost useless to spend your allocated practice time wishing that you weren't practising.

(b) Having *decided* to practise, make it difficult. Like a pest inspector, examine every corner of your tone and technique for flaws and practise to remove them. Only by this method will you improve quickly. After glancing through this book, you will see that many of the exercises are simply a way of looking at the same problem from different angles. You will not find it difficult to invent new ways.

(c) Try always to practise what you *can't* play. Don't indulge in too much self-flattery by playing through what you can already do well.

(d) As many of the exercises are taxing, be sure your posture and hand positions are correct. It is important to consult a good teacher on these points (see page 9).

GUARANTEE

Possession of this book is no guarantee that you will improve on the flute; there is no magic in the printed paper. But, if you have the desire to play well and put in some reasonable practice, you cannot fail to improve. It is simply a question of *time, patience* and *intelligent work*. The book is designed to avoid unnecessary practice. It is concentrated stuff. *Provided* that you follow the instructions carefully, you should make more than twice the improvement in half the time! *That is the guarantee.*

TO THE TEACHER

This is one of a series of basic exercise books for players of all ages who have been learning from about a year up to and including music college standard. There are some recommended speeds, but these should be chosen to accommodate the ability of the player. It was written for both amateur and would-be professional players. Some exercises are more difficult than others: take what you feel your pupils need.

TREVOR WYE 1986

TONE—I

QUALITY AND COLOUR

It has long been recognised that the cavities of the head, the throat, mouth and nasal cavities influence the tone of the flute player. It seems that the initial sound formed at the embouchure hole is reflected back into the mouth. Sound can travel very much faster than the air stream being emitted by the lips.
Don't imagine that increasing the size of any cavity in the mouth or throat will immediately cure your problems. Some initial experiments have to be done first.

Take a jam-jar and sing a glissando scale into it; at some point, the air in the jar will resonate in sympathy with the sung note. A jar, two-and-five-quarters larger won't necessarily increase the size of the sung note or in any way influence it. It might, it might not. First read the section on Posture in this book with particular reference to the position of the head and shoulders. See also Practice Book 5, the section on Breathing.

Take up your flute and play Exercise 1 in Practice Book 1—TONE, page 7. Keep your shoulders down and head up without appearing to pose for a military photograph. As you play the exercise, slightly and gently, yawn. This should (a) increase the cavity at the back of the mouth and throat and (b) allow the nasal cavity to influence the sound. Don't be surprised if something good happens to your tone, or nothing happens at all. You are changing but one factor which can influence tone production. The lips and head-joint position may also need minor changes in order to find the right *recipe* for you (see section on Embouchure). *Play each note of the pair for as long as possible.* Now make the vowel sounds, a, e, i, o, u, whilst holding each chromatic note. The purpose of all this is for you to experience any changes in tone colour or quality. It might be a few days before you recognise any change as being for the better, but when, and if, this happens, don't move. Repeat the note again and again so that you can recognise what it is that you are doing and be able to repeat it. Remember not to prod notes. (Practice Book 1, page 7, para 2) Play each note for a long time and *slowly* make throat, mouth, or vowel sound changes.
It will be valuable to spend a week or two trying these experiments during your tone practice.

Now move on to Practice Book 1—TONE, page 10, exercise (d), the Aquarium. Find a good 'recipe' (mouth, throat vowel sound, embouchure) for the A and G sharp. Observe what happens when descending to D. From bar five, the exercise descends slowly to D; use that part of it to discover what changes in the 'recipe' you need to make in order to get D *with the same colour as* A and G sharp. This may take time.
Experiment also, in the same key, with the Ravel tune, 2, (c). Here, an *entirely different* colour is required.
You will have observed by this time that for some sounds and some notes, the *cavity has to become smaller.* If it does, it only applies to *you* and not necessarily to anyone else; it's *your* private 'recipe'. It must be pointed out that you are always listening to yourself from a distance of a few inches; a good teacher, or a friend - they should be the same person! - can help by observing and commenting upon the sounds that you make. A tape recorder, too, can help.
Try to make the maximum *difference* in tone quality between the two D minor tunes. Then go on to practise in other keys, keeping that difference.

The next stage is to make the same experiments both with Practice Book 1—TONE, page 17, Exercise 12, and with the Tone Colour Exercise on page 24. Do all 24 keys. Remember to make the *maximum difference* in tone colour between keys.
Finally, on to page 18, the High Register: read the first few sentences. Your 'recipe' will help you to avoid sounding 'thin and squeaky'.
After that Flexibility, page 28, to enable you to move around in larger intervals.

Don't forget to check your intonation - nothing is usable *unless it can be played in tune.*

TONE—II

EMBOUCHURE

An impossible task, to try to describe what problems might arise with your embouchure. What can be done is to describe common complaints and problems and to suggest some remedies. It must be stressed that a good teacher is really indispensable, though some experimenting can be done by yourself if you are unable to consult a teacher.

The first and most common problem is turning the head-joint in too far. If you don't know whether you are, then see if the picture that follows describes you:

> The tone is small and often cloyingly sweet; it is much thinner in the third octave; there is little variation in loudness; it varies between *mf* and *pp*; soft sounds, in fact, very soft sounds, are easy; it is difficult to be heard above the piano unless the lid is shut; other players sound stronger; the head-joint has to be pushed right in and even then it's sometimes flat.

If most of these things apply to you then *turn out*. More than that, *pull out and turn out*.
The reason why all players have a leaning toward turning in is that (a) octave playing is easier, (b) the upper notes are easier, (c) *pp* is easier and (d) it avoids or diminishes any air-escape, or hiss, in the tone.
All of these problems can be overcome with practice, let there be no mistake about that. All of these four reasons are true, and do produce the described effect, but are an easy option. What needs to be looked at are the disadvantages: (a) an often inaudible sound, (b) no variation in dynamics, (c) no real *forte*, (d) great intonation problems and (e) little or no variation in colour.

If, having read that, you decide to experiment, *don't expect immediate results*. The suggestions which follow should, however, begin to work in a week or two.

Firstly the *size* of the tone is affected by the amount the embouchure hole is uncovered. The more it is uncovered, the larger the tone. The more it is uncovered, the louder the tone. The more it is uncovered, the more air is needed. So, start by playing the exercises in Practice Book 1—TONE, pages 7-9, with the head-joint pulled out about ⅜ of an inch (about 10 m.m.) more than you usually have it. This will also flatten the the scale, so now roll the head-joint out a bit to sharpen it. Try, for the first few days, not to cover more than half of the hole. *Don't let your hands roll it back in again.* See how far the hole *can* be uncovered. Always play *forte*. You will lose a lot of air; the sound will be coarse; the pitch may be difficult to control; it may be difficult to play in the second octave; there's a lot of hiss; you are out of breath for comparatively short notes. *Fine!* It's going to take time. *The size and volume of tone is directly proportional to (a) the amount the hole is covered and (b) to the natural cavities of the head. (see TONE—I in this book.)*

A couple of weeks on pages 7-9, in Practice Book 1, and you should now progress to pages 13 and 14 only, followed by exercise 12 on page 17. *Do not try to play softly at this stage.* You will by now be making quite a different sound than your previous dwarfish tone but possibly with two problems: (a) too much air is used and (b) it is difficult to play softly, especially in the second octave. Intervals may also be difficult. Good. Now go back to the first exercises again and find the 'recipe' which allows you to make *the same volume of sound with half the amount of air*. That's all. It will take time but you should find this 'recipe' in a week or two. You will also find that all but one of the problems enumerated in paragraph 3 have evaporated – playing softly. Back to Practice Book 1—TONE, pages 34-36. Take time to do these properly, particularly pages 35 and 36. Note-Endings are a way of learning the 'recipe' for keeping the pitch constant whilst playing both loudly and softly. *Move your head* if *pp* is flat and you have reached the limit of movement of *both* jaw and lips. Thereafter practise page 24 – Tone Colour Exercise - *in all 24 keys*, both *very* loudly and *very* softly. It's all a question of _____ , _____ and _____ _____ .
When your embouchure has settled down, practise the section in this book on The Top Register, playing softly. The rest is up to you.

TONE-III

WARMING UP BEFORE PRACTICE

An athlete has to do an hour or two in the gym doing work-outs to tone up his muscles and to get them working for him. We don't need anything like that time to warm up, but we do *need* to warm up. The athlete would never attempt a flat-out race from cold without thoroughly warming up: it is the same for the lips with regard to the flute. They are a complex group of muscles and need proper care if you are to subject them to difficult and lengthy tone and flexibility exercises. It's crazy to start the day by rushing around the compass, particularly at the top end. A good warm-up need only take 10-15 minutes but will allow you to play for longer at the end of the day without becoming tense or strained.

When warming up, keep to the low register for the first few minutes. It's not important what you play, just so long as you enjoy it. Avoid octave playing. Start with something of this kind:

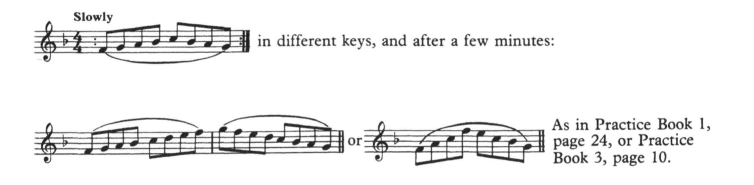

in different keys, and after a few minutes:

or

As in Practice Book 1, page 24, or Practice Book 3, page 10.

Little by little, explore the second octave. If your lips feel strong, go on to the lower part of the third octave; if not, stay where you are.

Now, after a few more minutes, practise simple intervals to gain flexibility, such as:

As in Practice Book 1, page 25.

And, if your lips really are in good shape, as they should be after a few days if you follow this advice, then go on to the Flexibility Exercise in Practice Book 1, page 28.

Don't run too fast, too soon.

POSTURE

BODY AND HAND POSITIONS

Why is this subject to be found in an Advanced Practice Book? Simply because it's the most frequently recurring problem that teachers, at whatever level of teaching, have to contend with. A poor posture negatively affects breathing, tone and technique to a large degree. So much so that many of the difficulties experienced by the beginner and advanced student alike would not have occurred, or, at the very least, would not have been 'problems', if the correct posture had been observed and adhered to in the first place.*

But we are not machines. During a player's performing life, he has to cope with uncomfortable chairs, orchestral seating positions, chamber music placement, concert platform positions, the stress of trying-to-get-it-right and many other factors. All these can encourage a less productive posture and, even for professional performers, may need re-adjustment from time to time.

First, posture: standing is the most common position for practising and should be looked at first. Stand, feet apart, with the weight slightly forward. Not so much that your thigh muscles become tight, but enough to keep off your heels. Don't bend your leg; this tilts the pelvis and can affect breathing. Next, hold the flute to your front as if it were an oboe, then turn your head to the left as if looking round your shoulder. Now bring your flute up into blowing position without (a) raising the shoulders or (b) *bringing your head to the flute*. Return to the normal head-front flute-down position and repeat this sequence, turning your head and raising the flute together, several times. Note that the body is facing in a *different direction to the head*. Repeat this now, standing in front of a music stand. Your body will have to face to the *right* of the stand for your head to be square on to it. This may not feel entirely comfortable for a while, but it will encourage *quicker progress* in all the difficult exercises you have to practise.

When a beginner first takes up a flute, he has no idea whether he is going to be a roaring genius or just a tolerable amateur. If the correct posture is adopted from the very start, at least he has given his body every chance to contribute to his possible success.

When a householder has an extension built on to his house, the Local Authority requires him to lay foundations suitable for a height of *at least two stories*: The householder may, in time, want to add another floor. He may insist that he doesn't want to, and never will, but he *may* change his mind. So may the next owner of the house.

When starting out on the flute, the beginner should lay sufficiently strong foundations to suit all eventualities whether or not he thinks he's going to be a genius or a duffer.

Which brings us to hand positions,* vis-a-vis the flute.

Let your right hand drop limply to your side. Raise your arm so as to observe your fingers. Your thumb is positioned sideways to your fingers. Only by twisting your thumb – and thus making the hand tense – can the flat part of the tip of the thumb be in contact with the tip of the finger. If this is the *natural* relaxed position of the thumb – as when asleep – then this is the position which must be used in flute playing.

Holding the flute directly in front of your chest, that is, not in the playing position, place your right hand fingers on the keys. Don't let your thumb position itself yet. Now, allow the thumb to find a place on the flute which is as near as possible to the position in which it most naturally falls and there you are! The fingers are gently curved, including the little finger. But, and this is where the problems start, *slowly* push the flute away from you into playing position. Remember to turn your head. The thumb probably begins to turn until it is *flat* on the flute; the fingers may also turn until the little finger is straight. O.K., then you know what to do about it; turn the wrist and arm slightly to maintain the relaxed position even when the flute is in playing position. If your little finger is bent 'inwards' – a very common problem! – bend it back into the relaxed curved position. The same with the fingers; they too should be curved.

Do not practise any difficult technical exercises with a bad right hand posture. All exercises must be tackled with a correct posture. If your hand position was previously bad, you may have a couple of weeks of hell. Demolishing your one-storied extension and re-digging out the foundations would also be hell, if not to your back then certainly to your pocket.

* *The correct posture for beginners is set out clearly in* A Beginners Practice Book for the Flute – *Trevor Wye (Novello) 1984, and in* Proper Flute Playing – *Trevor Wye (Novello) 1987.*

* *These, too, are clearly illustrated in* A Beginners Practice Book for the Flute – *Trevor Wye (Novello) 1984.*

Don't start worrying about hand positions when *performing*, just make sure that all private practice is done in this way. In time it will become part of your natural, relaxed posture.

The left hand: same thing, relaxed curved fingers, *including the little finger*, but this hand has also to support the flute. Tuck your hand well under so that the index finger, where it joins on to the hand, is underneath the flute and capable of *lifting it up*. Using the finger to press the head-joint against your mouth is not enough. It must lift, and so prevent the flute slipping when perspiration attacks your lower lip during an important concert. Your thumb must now be straight and may feel odd, and a C sharp trill may be slower; both can be overcome by practice. The advantages far outweigh the disadvantages.

An open hole flute has two advantages only; (a) it encourages a correct hand position, (b) it gives some extra fingerings.

If you follow this advice carefully from *today*, your progress after the initial 2-3 weeks, will be greatly increased. Guaranteed! You will have allowed yourself the option of a tower block and not just a garden shed.

TECHNIQUE—I

ADVANCED TECHNICAL EXERCISES

Most technical exercises seem to cause tension in the fingers or hand. Although a certain amount of tension probably should be felt, too much causes difficulties in technical passages for the rest of that day.

These exercises have been devised to enable all combinations of *finger movement* to be covered each day without causing strain, provided that the hand positions are correct. (See the section on Posture)

PRACTICE NOTES

1 Set your metronome to a speed at which you can play through A B C D *almost* comfortably. When possible, increase the speed a little every few days.

2 As long as you can play each bar *four times*, don't worry if the notes aren't *even*. You are asked simply to be able to *play each bar four times non-stop*. That's all. They will become even in time, so *don't stop to practise* a particular bar unless it is *really* poor.

3 As you become familiar with the patterns and find you can play some bars easily, then play those bars once only. It saves time.

4 Be sure to use the correct fingering:
    (i) use R.H. little finger down at the *start* of E.
    (ii) use 3rd finger for F♯.
    (iii) play B♭ fingered the 'long' way, with 1st finger R.H.
    (iv) make sure that the 1st finger of the left hand is off for D♮ and E♭.

5 Study the charts below.

How to practise for the first month:

DAY ONE	A	B	C	D	Q	R
DAY TWO	I	J	K	L	Q	S
DAY THREE	A	B	C	D	Q	T
DAY FOUR	I	J	K	L	Q	R
DAY FIVE	A	B	C	D	Q	S
DAY SIX	I	J	K	L	Q	T
DAY SEVEN	Scales, as in Practice Book 5.					

From the first month onwards:

DAY ONE	A	B	C	D	Q	R	DAY EIGHT	E	F	G	H	Q	R
DAY TWO	I	J	K	L	Q	S	DAY NINE	M	N	O	P	Q	S
DAY THREE	E	F	G	H	Q	T	DAY TEN	A	B	C	D	Q	T
DAY FOUR	M	N	O	P	Q	R	DAY ELEVEN	I	J	K	L	Q	R
DAY FIVE	A	B	C	D	Q	S	DAY TWELVE	E	F	G	H	Q	S
DAY SIX	I	J	K	L	Q	T	DAY THIRTEEN	M	N	O	P	Q	T
DAY SEVEN	Scales as in Practice Book 5						DAY FOURTEEN	Scales					

As your technique improves, you may be able to get through A B C D with E F G H, not forgetting Q plus an R, S or T.

If there is a weakness in one hand or finger in particular, see the section Technique II, 26 Digital Exercises.

When you start the two-week chart, aim for evenness, speed and metronomic accuracy, though read again practice note 2, above.

Be sure your posture and hand positions are correct.

Don't stint yourself on the Exercises: '*Nothing succeeds like excess*'. (Oscar Wilde)

Don't continue to practise if pain is felt; check on your posture and hand positions.

TECHNIQUE—I

ADVANCED TECHNICAL EXERCISES

A *Repeat each bar four times*

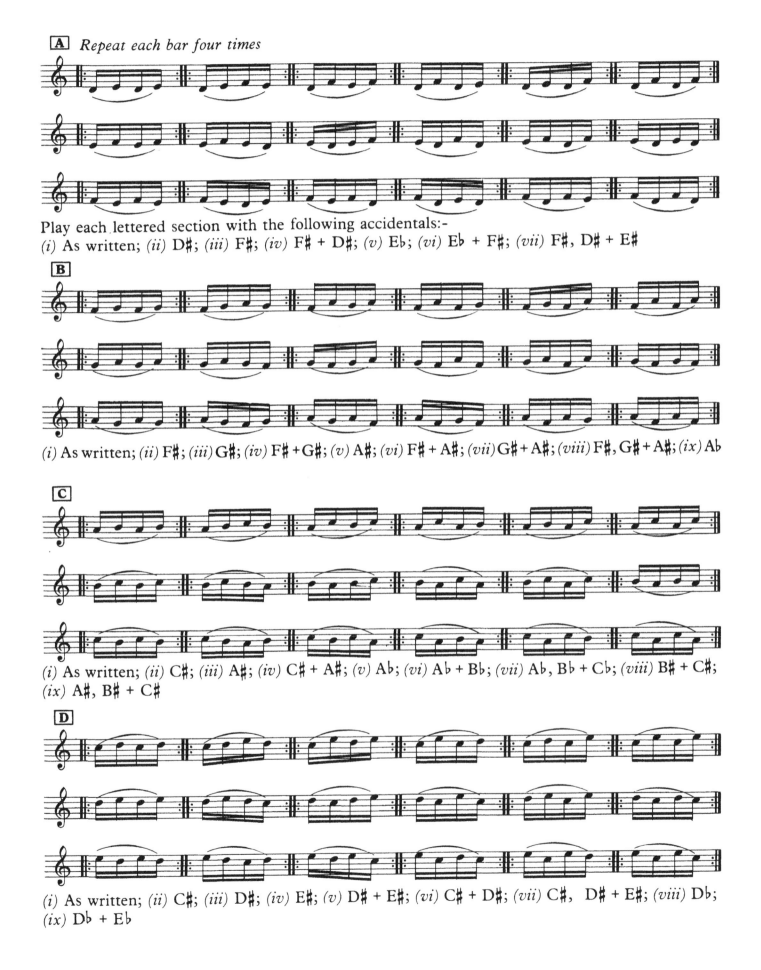

Play each lettered section with the following accidentals:-
(i) As written; *(ii)* D♯; *(iii)* F♯; *(iv)* F♯ + D♯; *(v)* E♭; *(vi)* E♭ + F♯; *(vii)* F♯, D♯ + E♯

B

(i) As written; *(ii)* F♯; *(iii)* G♯; *(iv)* F♯ + G♯; *(v)* A♯; *(vi)* F♯ + A♯; *(vii)* G♯ + A♯; *(viii)* F♯, G♯ + A♯; *(ix)* A♭

C

(i) As written; *(ii)* C♯; *(iii)* A♯; *(iv)* C♯ + A♯; *(v)* A♭; *(vi)* A♭ + B♭; *(vii)* A♭, B♭ + C♭; *(viii)* B♯ + C♯; *(ix)* A♯, B♯ + C♯

D

(i) As written; *(ii)* C♯; *(iii)* D♯; *(iv)* E♯; *(v)* D♯ + E♯; *(vi)* C♯ + D♯; *(vii)* C♯, D♯ + E♯; *(viii)* D♭; *(ix)* D♭ + E♭

(i) As written; *(ii)* A♭; *(iii)* G♭; *(iv)* A♭ + G♭; *(v)* D♭ + A♭; *(vi)* A♯; *(vii)* D♯ + A♯; *(viii)* G♯ + A♯

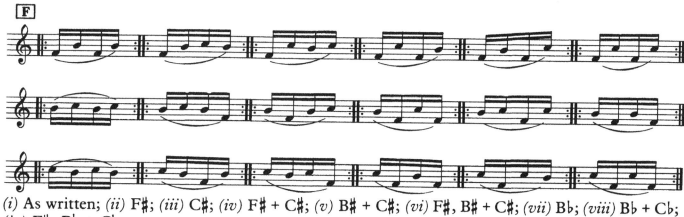

(i) As written; *(ii)* F♯; *(iii)* C♯; *(iv)* F♯ + C♯; *(v)* B♯ + C♯; *(vi)* F♯, B♯ + C♯; *(vii)* B♭; *(viii)* B♭ + C♭;
(ix) F♯, B♭ + C♭

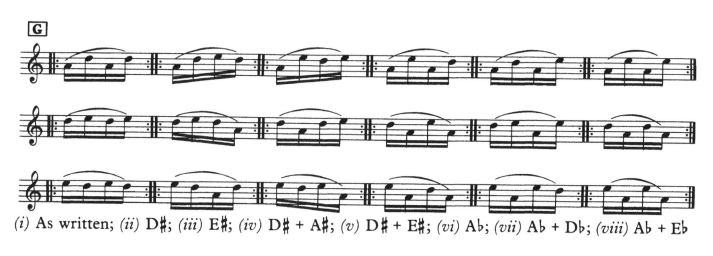

(i) As written; *(ii)* D♯; *(iii)* E♯; *(iv)* D♯ + A♯; *(v)* D♯ + E♯; *(vi)* A♭; *(vii)* A♭ + D♭; *(viii)* A♭ + E♭

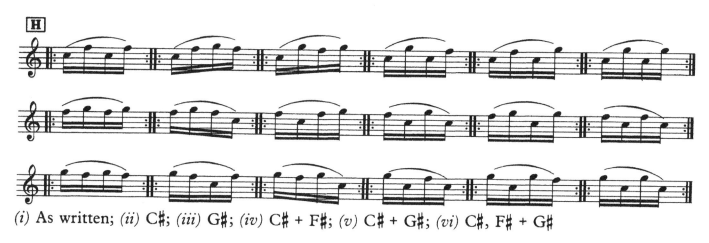

(i) As written; *(ii)* C♯; *(iii)* G♯; *(iv)* C♯ + F♯; *(v)* C♯ + G♯; *(vi)* C♯, F♯ + G♯

I

(i) As written; *(ii)* E♭; *(iii)* G♭; *(iv)* E♭ + G♭; *(v)* E♭, F♭ + G♭; *(vi)* F♯; *(vii)* G♯; *(viii)* F♯ + G♯

J

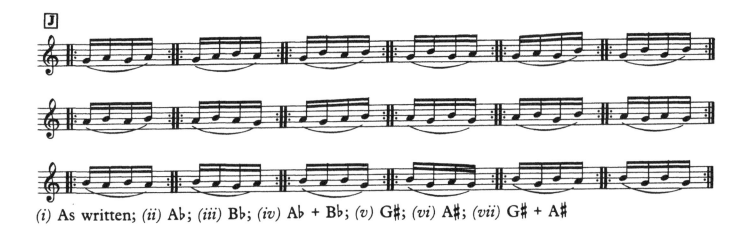

(i) As written; *(ii)* A♭; *(iii)* B♭; *(iv)* A♭ + B♭; *(v)* G♯; *(vi)* A♯; *(vii)* G♯ + A♯

K

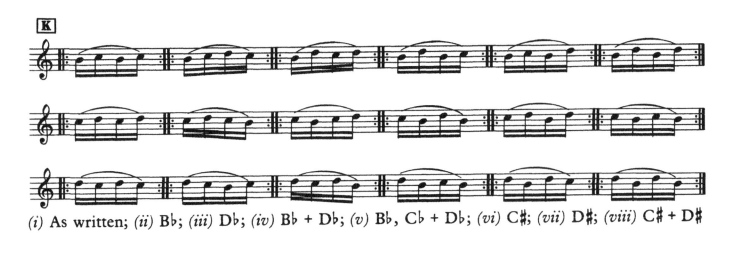

(i) As written; *(ii)* B♭; *(iii)* D♭; *(iv)* B♭ + D♭; *(v)* B♭, C♭ + D♭; *(vi)* C♯; *(vii)* D♯; *(viii)* C♯ + D♯

L

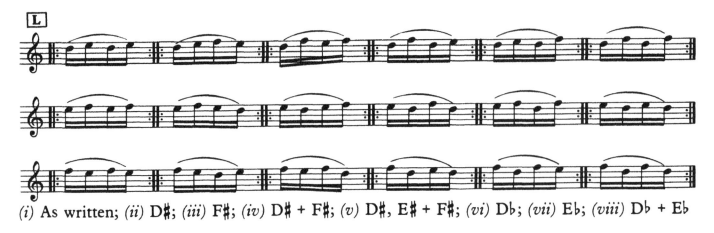

(i) As written; *(ii)* D♯; *(iii)* F♯; *(iv)* D♯ + F♯; *(v)* D♯, E♯ + F♯; *(vi)* D♭; *(vii)* E♭; *(viii)* D♭ + E♭

M

(i) As written; *(ii)* E♭; *(iii)* A♭; *(iv)* E♭ + A♭; *(v)* B♭; *(vi)* E♭ + B♭; *(vii)* E♭, A♭+ B♭; *(viii)* A♯

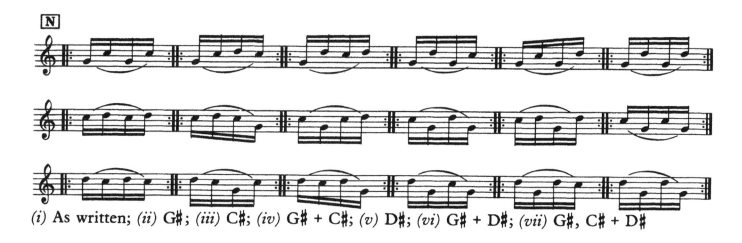

N

(i) As written; *(ii)* G♯; *(iii)* C♯; *(iv)* G♯ + C♯; *(v)* D♯; *(vi)* G♯ + D♯; *(vii)* G♯, C♯ + D♯

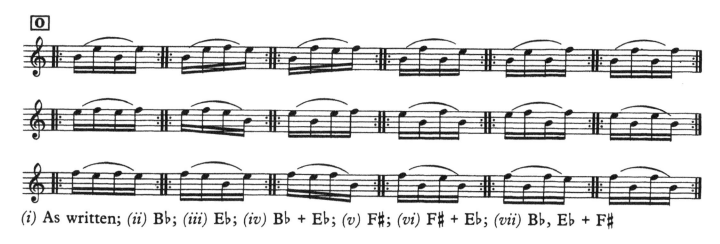

O

(i) As written; *(ii)* B♭; *(iii)* E♭; *(iv)* B♭ + E♭; *(v)* F♯; *(vi)* F♯ + E♭; *(vii)* B♭, E♭ + F♯

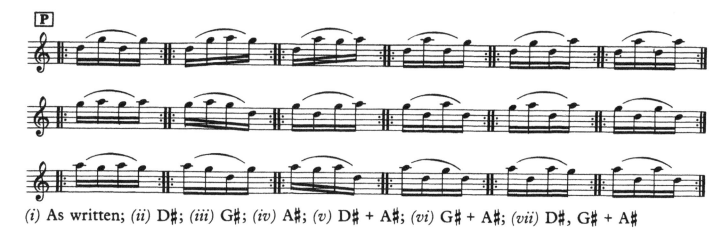

P

(i) As written; *(ii)* D♯; *(iii)* G♯; *(iv)* A♯; *(v)* D♯ + A♯; *(vi)* G♯ + A♯; *(vii)* D♯, G♯ + A♯

(i) As written (ii) C♯; (iii) D♯; (iv) E♭; (v) C♯ + D♯

(i) As written (ii) D♭; (iii) D♭ + E♭; (iv) D♭, E♭ + F♯

R Play each bar 4 times

S x 4

T x 4

How to practise the chromatic exercises R, S and T:

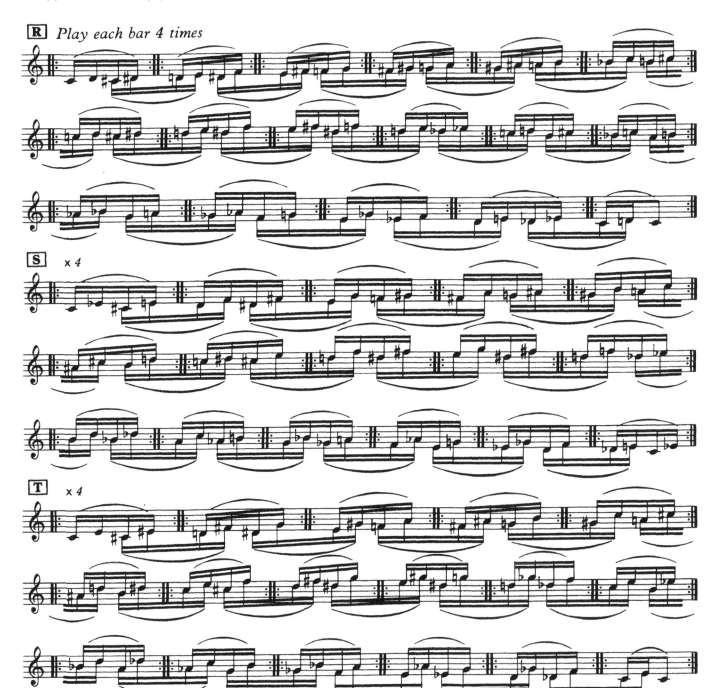

TECHNIQUE—II

26 DIGITAL EXERCISES

The following exercises are for specific weaknesses in any finger, the thumb, or either hand.
First, read the section on Posture (page 9). Keep your hands *still* whilst practising these exercises, particularly the right hand when the little finger is in use. Use a mirror to check yourself.
Each bar is to be repeated four times. Be rhythmic. Play them as fast as you rhythmically can. Use a metronome. Don't work for more than a few minutes on one finger - give it a rest and go back to it later. You may well have to start slowly as they are not easy. They were not written to torture you, nor were they simply written to be difficult; rather they are designed to achieve independence of finger movement, which in itself is difficult.
The exercises are also designed for the 3rd octave; see the section The Top Register—II, Technique, in this book (page 27).
Draw a circle in red around those letters you find really difficult; every fourth day, practise only these.
Press on!

RIGHT HAND
Little finger

Third finger

Second and third fingers

18

Second finger

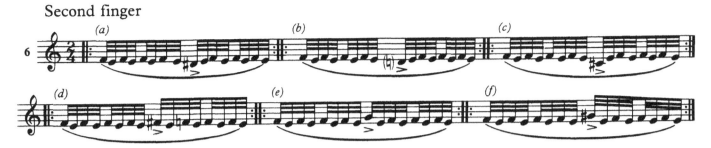

First finger

COMPLETE RIGHT HAND

LEFT HAND
Little finger

Third finger

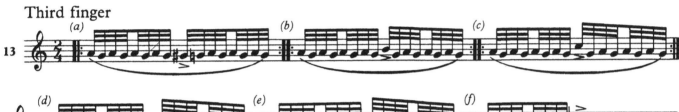

Second finger

20

Thumb

First finger

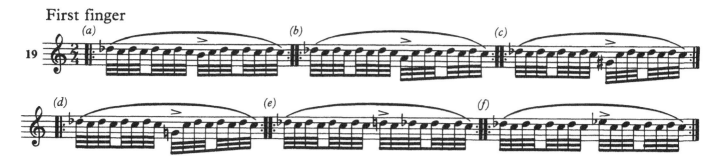

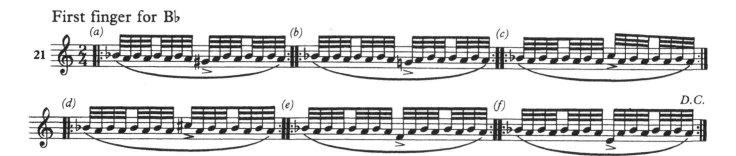

First finger for B♭

TWO HANDS TOGETHER

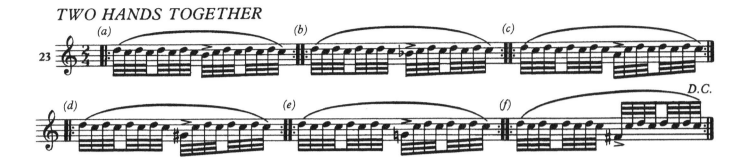

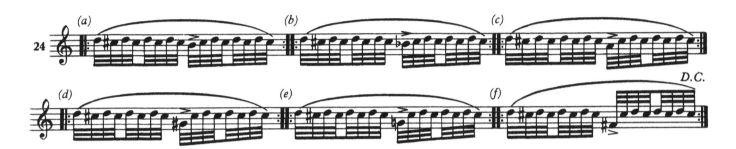

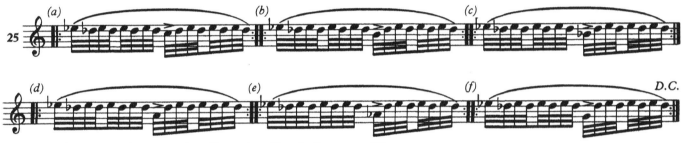

Finger E♭ correctly: see also Practice Book 3, page 29.

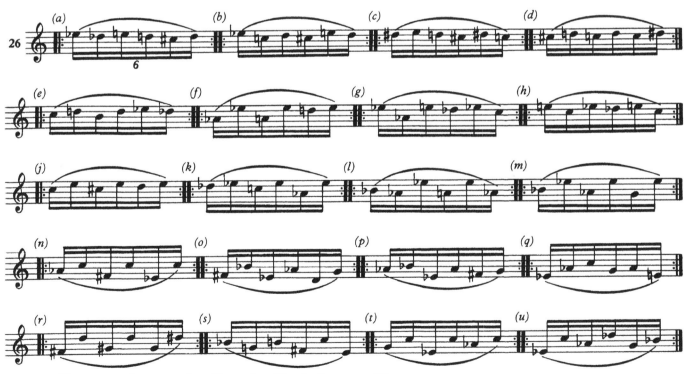

Finger E♭ correctly: see also Practice Book 3, page 29.

LARGER INTERVALS

Although some mixed intervals have already appeared in the foregoing exercises, end each day with a play-through of the following. Only stop and practise them if great difficulty is experienced. It is sufficient to be able to play each bar four times without stopping, even though they may be a little untidy.

Be sure to use all correct fingerings, i.e. little finger for E & F, and the 'long' B♭.

TECHNIQUE—III

RAPID SCALES AND ARPEGGIOS

Most players, at Practice Book 6 level, will have little trouble playing scale and arpeggio passages in a rhythmic and controlled way. To increase the speed further, especially in the third octave, seems elusive! The reason is that too much is attempted at one time; in these exercises, the player takes short steps at a speed he chooses.

Exercise 1. Start slowly; *squash* the grace note against the following note. *Finger every note correctly;* use your D♯ key for E♮. When this has been mastered at ♩ = 60, push the metronome speed up a notch or two and begin again. Don't play the next bar until the previous one is *absolutely perfect in every way* – the fingering, evenness, and speed of the small notes. Keep your fingers close to the keys.

Check:
*   Are there any notes missing?
*   Are you fingering correctly? If you do cheat, you cheat yourself. O.K.?
*   Are the rapid scales *even*?
*   Are they *rapid* scales?
*   Are you keeping your fingers close to the keys?
*   Read the section on *posture* again.

Apply this principle to all scales, arpeggios and to any difficult passages you may come across.

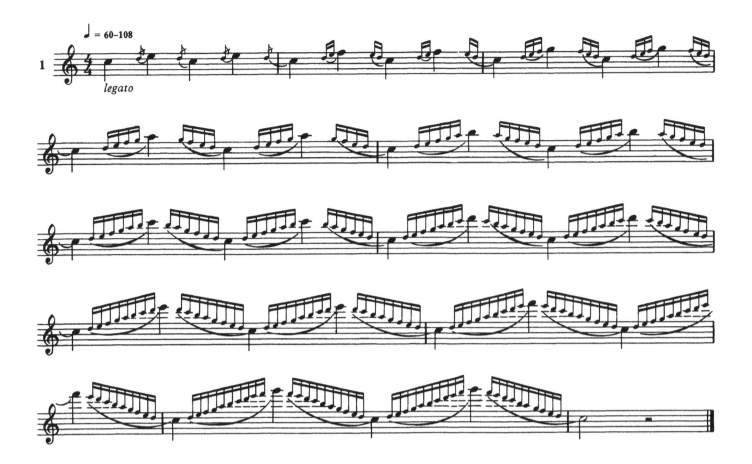

Now practise in different keys. Choose more difficult keys as your technique improves.

Apply the same principle to arpeggios. It's another method of acquiring a fast, even technique. It's all a question of _____,_____, and _____, as usual.

These are more tiring for the lips and should be practised only when thoroughly warmed up.

Finally, if you have tried many different key-signatures, you will want to play the more exotic varieties of arpeggio. It will be quickly understood that this is a method of overcoming a technical difficulty in a piece of flute music. Here are some examples:

which will eventually lead to:

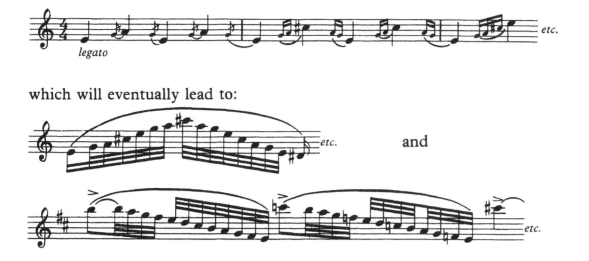

which you will recognise as parts of the Chaminade Concertino.

And now, practise the chromatic exercise which follows. Use different starting notes each day.

These exercises are by no means complete in the form set out above. Rather, they have been set out sketchily to stimulate your ideas on practising and not necessarily to form a complete exercise.

TONGUING BETWEEN THE LIPS

Different languages have different levels of clarity; O.K., all are usually clear to their own countrymen, but some are more clear. French is traditionally taught with a natural emphasis on the movement of the lips, tongue and throat. There is a great respect for clarity. On the other hand, compare this with some of the sloppy sentences you hear in the U.S.A. where words such as 'little' become 'lil' and mirror, meer. In the U.K. too, there are some regions where English sounds like a foreign language. Vive la difference, I say! But the lack of use of the tongue just happens to result in awful articulation on the flute, or none at all. French flautists are known for the excellent clarity of their articulation. We non-French can learn to do this too, but because of the various languages in which the tongue is used less than in French, we find it takes a bit longer and means a good bit more ————, —————— and —————— ——————!

Many young players are taught to articulate DE or DER.

The teacher sometimes makes a comparison between the clarity of articulation between DER, TER and THER, or DU and TU. Based on this, DER is by far the clearest and neatest. Because? It is further back in the mouth and nearer the place where the sound is produced.

The flute isn't played in the throat; it's in *front* of the tongue. Therefore tonguing nearer to where the sound is produced *should* give a more immediate start to a note and with less effort. It does.

Without the flute: whilst maintaining a flute embouchure, point the tongue between the lips and, stroking the *top* lip, withdraw it quickly. It 'pops'. Look in a mirror. Don't force your lips apart with the tongue; try to fill the 'blowhole' with the tip of your tongue. Remember to push it more toward the *top* lip. Take up your flute. Look in a mirror. Withdraw your tongue but *do not blow yet*. Repeat. Now 'pop' back the tongue, wait a full second, then blow:

POP . . . . HA.   POP . . . . HA.

Gradually shorten the interval between the two movements until the tongue just *begins* to 'touch' the start of the note. Maintain this balance for a few minutes. You should hear a pleasant 'POP' at the beginning of your note.

PROBLEMS

1 Don't move your lips or jaw during this operation.
2 Don't build up pressure behind your tongue or, when it is withdrawn, there will be an explosion. The front row of your audience will put up umbrellas.
3 Look in *a mirror*. You must be able to *see* your tongue. Just practise a few staccato notes to start with. Now turn to Practice Book 1—Tone, page 36, exercise 7. Play this slowly, staccato, and softly, ignoring the *f* and *p*. Practise this for a few days until you are used to the movement.

In the meantime, every time you pick up your flute, start the note off with the tongue, and, every time you take a breath in a piece of music, start again with the tongue forward.

Now: turn to Practice Book 3—Articulation, page 10, exercise A. Work at these 24 keys until ♩= 120 is reached. During this period you will salivate a lot; your salivary glands assume all this activity is because food is about! It may take a time to train it to think again. It's a common problem. After a couple of weeks, your articulation should begin to sound clear. Read back over the Problems. O.K.?

NEXT STEP

Start the single tonguing exercises from No. 5, page 12 and work through them. As you get faster *withdraw the movement of the tongue between the lips until it is between the teeth* for fast passage work. Remember 'THER'? For the next few months, use the tongue out or between the teeth for everything.

After these months, read again all the comments about single tonguing in the Articulation Book from page 10 onwards. Even with your other articulation, you were constantly reminded to tongue forwards. All of which means that you may *now* be in the position of having joined your two kinds of tonguing together, giving a wide variety of attack to suit whichever piece you are playing.

Now read pages 5-9 again in Practice Book 3 and you will see that there are many ways of varying your articulation *without using slurs*. Your palette should now have many colours. The rest is up to you.

THE TOP REGISTER—I

PLAYING SOFTLY

Whilst producing as near as possible a flute embouchure, blow up your nose. Cause a thin stream of air to hit the end of your nose at the *same air speed* as if you were playing top F. Now with the flute in position, repeat the above. Take a big breath and slowly, *very slowly*, lower this needle of air whilst fingering the third octave F♮. Don't worry if, half way down, you run out of air; just start again. *Remember the air speed.* When you get near to a note beginning to sound, slow the movement right down. A very quiet, but in tune or even SHARP note will appear. Stop. Think for a moment. Usually, when you play top F *very softly*, you are flat. This is because the air is raised up from a low position for fear of the F not sounding at all!

Take up your flute and repeat this many times. Now change to F♯ and after some minutes go to G, G♯, A, B♭ and B♮. *Provided that the air speed is right*, you should be able to play the top notes very softly with ease. If it doesn't work, you are too tense.

Now the difficult part:
Repeat the last few notes of the top octave – say from G♮ up – this time trying to let your lips and jaw slacken. Don't relax completely or there will be no embouchure.
Repeat this experiment every day for several days, until you become good at 'catching' *pp* top notes. If ever difficulty is experienced, it is usually because the air speed is too slow.
Turn to Practice Book 1—TONE, page 22. Read it. Turn to page 18, start on exercise A, No. 1, but *reverse* the nuances, starting *piano*. After a week or two, go to page 20, always reversing the nuances printed. Spend half your available time on these two pages but finish your practice with page 28 – Flexibility—I. Play the first six lines of the Sousseman study, repeating back to the beginning and always softly. Quite softly, or very softly, or even very very softly? *As softly as you reasonably can without becoming tense.* On a bad day, you may not be able to play softly at all. Don't worry. Don't be dictated to by this book! Do only what your lips will allow you to do.
Repeat with variations A to I.

THE TOP REGISTER—II

TECHNIQUE

These are tiring for the lips, therefore, practise them only at the end of a practice session.
Even when playing exercises slowly, move the fingers *quickly* and precisely. Start with Practice Book II—Technique, on page 8, and start at the sign *. Don't wait until these are perfect, but when you can play most of them at ♩ = 72 practise the Scale Exercises on page 14. Again when they are all about ♩ = 72, and most mistakes have been put right, go on to the Machiavellian Exercises II, from No. 1 to No. 26, an octave higher.
The foregoing exercises are to ensure you have a basic technique of the fingers to enable you to tackle the advanced technical exercises in this book. The earlier preparation on Practice Book 2 will save both your lip, brain, and sometimes your patience, when trying these advanced exercises. Finally, don't do too much of these in the first days. Build some strength in your lips day by day.

For more advanced players start with the Advanced Technical Exercises in this book, K, D and L one octave higher, followed by A, B, I and J two octaves higher. Don't attempt all seven sections in one day; it is too tiring for the lips – and ears. Do what you can in 20 minutes. Do a further 10-15 minutes after an interval of 2+ hours. Now read the Guarantee in the front of this book.
After some weeks of practice, turn to 26 Digital Exercises Nos. 1, 3, 4, 6, and 8, two octaves higher; later still, when your technique allows, practise nos. 2, 5, 7, 9, and 10, also two octaves higher. Thereafter, extend your practice to 11, 12, 14 and 16.

THE TOP REGISTER—III

SHARPNESS IN TOP REGISTER

If you don't think this section applies to you, think again! Only a few very remarkable international virtuosi are usually – at least, most of the time – free of this problem. If you are still not sure, then you may have a poor sense of pitch. To check yourself, use a battery operated pitch meter; fix the pitch at 440 or 442 or whatever pitch you normally play at, and tune your A♮'s and D♮'s to this. Try to get someone to switch the notes from one to another for you as you play in the top register. WELL? Pretty devastating, isn't it? The cork can be moved out a little but this will affect the *tone* of the flute throughout its compass. *Leave the cork alone.*

Turn to Practice Book 1, page 13, 2nd paragraph: 'Don't raise the airstream too high when ascending . . . . . ' Also page 18: 'Don't raise the air stream too much . . . . . '

This sums up part of the problem but not all of it. Raising the air stream makes tone production of the third octave easier, and sharp. The third octave is in any case sharper because of the increased air speed.

In general, then, try to keep the air stream, that is, the direction in which you blow, as low as possible. You will find that your tone *sounds better* like that.

Start with Practice Book 1—TONE, page 17, Ex. 12. Whilst ascending from A to E, *don't raise the airstream*. Yes, you were taught that at the beginning, to help you get the note. Now you've got it, lower the air direction again. This may cause the note to split. O.K. Find out how long you can direct the air without it splitting. Spend a good amount of time on these exercises.

Now turn to page 18 in the same book, The High Register. Continue practising in the same manner for the third octave, only here use the following fingerings; they will flatten the sharpest notes in addition to the work which *you* are doing with the airstream. Consider them as standard fingerings from now on and incorporate them into your daily scales and arpeggios.

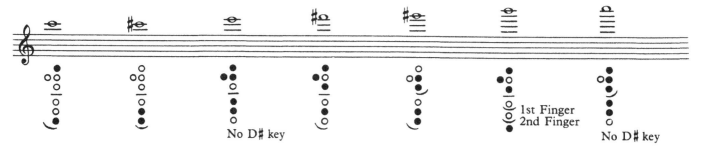

There is a fingering for the notoriously sharp top E♭ but it isn't practicable for fast passagework, though it can be used in tunes.

Check all your new fingerings with a tuning meter. From here on, the standard fingering chart rules which have governed your playing till now no longer apply. If it works, use it.

TOP REGISTER—IV

SPECIAL FINGERINGS

Most of these are for special occasions and will get you out of trouble in many pieces from the standard repertoire, both in orchestral and solo playing.

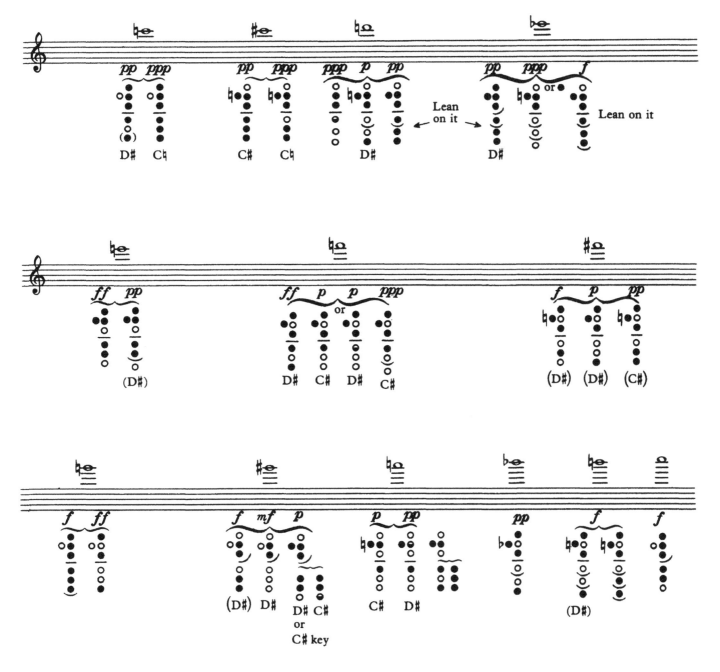

☉: Partially cover the hole

Lean on it: partially, or completely open the trill key.

(D♯) is a flatter fingering.

THE TOP REGISTER-V
A TRILL CHART

SEMITONES

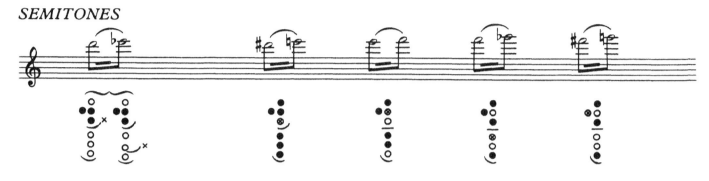

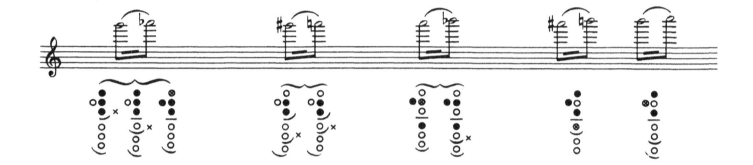

TONES

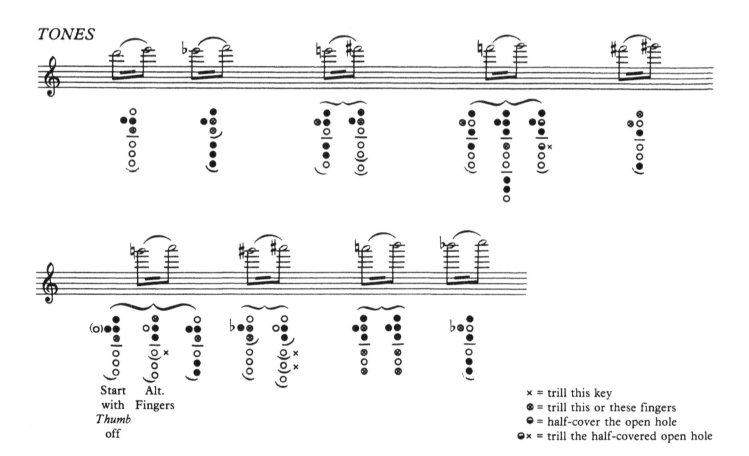

Start Alt.
with Fingers
Thumb
off

× = trill this key
⊗ = trill this or these fingers
◐ = half-cover the open hole
◐× = trill the half-covered open hole

THE TOP REGISTER—VI

FOURTH OCTAVE EXERCISES

The top notes of the 4th octave.
Practice of these notes can be even more tiring; try them for no more than a few minutes at a time. After a few days the lips will become a little stronger and be more capable of holding an 'embouchure'.
Some advice on getting the notes easily:

(a) Don't turn the flute in; just the reverse, keep it turned out.
(b) Try each new note as a short, fortissimo, burst of air.
(c) Make sure you try out all the available fingerings. Some are easier on some flutes, difficult on others.
(d) Remember your neighbours.
(e) Leave E♭ out until you've worked at the others.*

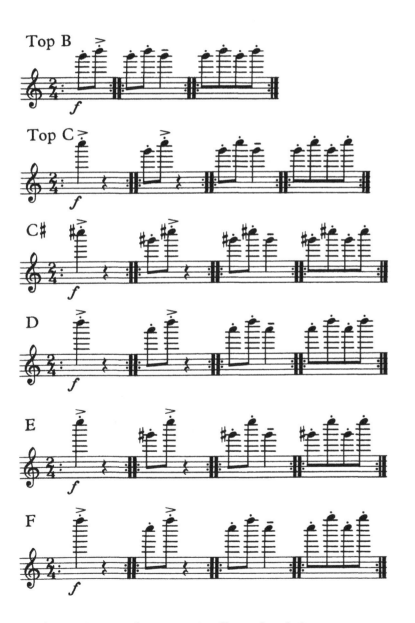

* E♭ has been left out as the fingering is by no means standard and it tends to be more difficult on some flutes than others. Try it later.

THE TOP NOTES

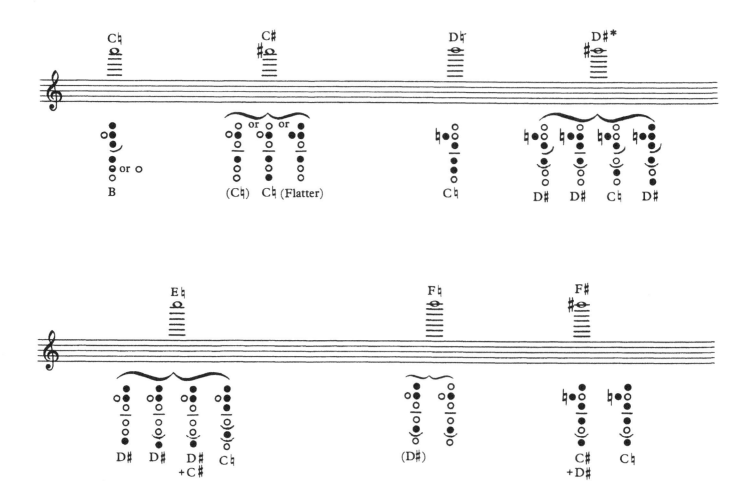

* Try D♯ later: it's more difficult.

FOURTH OCTAVE EXERCISES

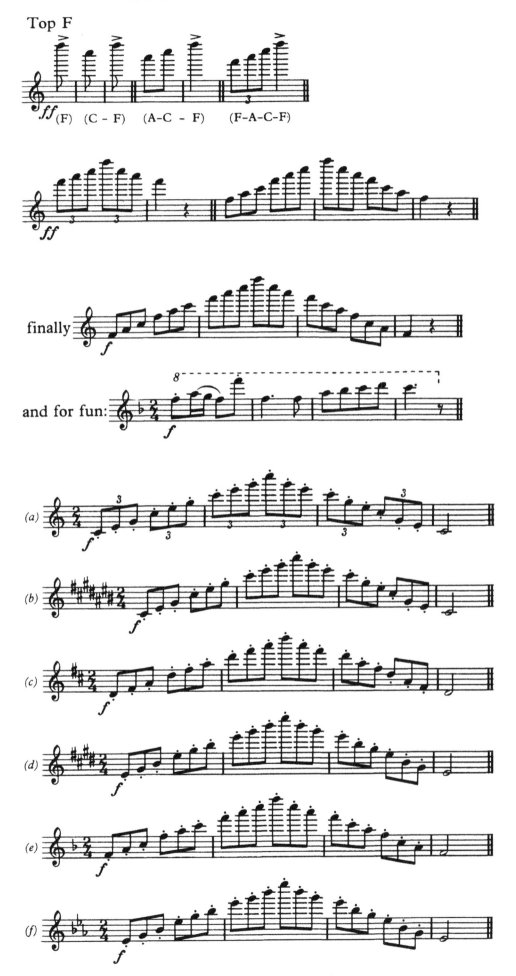

BREATHING

CIRCULAR BREATHING

Do not consider this section to be in any way essential to your development as a flute player. It's in this book for fun. It is also considered by contemporary music experts to be necessary for this music. The information is here: you must choose whether or not to use it.

Circular Breathing is so called because the air is drawn in through the nose *whilst still blowing* and whilst still playing an uninterrupted note with the mouth. Magic? No. New? No. It's been going on for thousands of years. To glass blowers, it's a normal part of technique. Difficult? Not really. It just *sounds* difficult. Puff out your cheeks: make a small hole between your lips and *slowly* allow the air to escape. It makes a squeaking sound. Notice that the back of your tongue is against the top of the back of your mouth, which prevents the air in your lungs from contributing to the air supply. Now take a glass half filled with water and a plastic drinking straw. Squeeze the drinking straw half way down so as to create some 'resistance'. Blow down it using *only* the air in your cheeks. The air gets used up in a couple of seconds. Practise economising to extend the continuous air flow to a count of 4 (♩ = 60). Don't go on until you can do this easily.

Next step: Whilst performing your four-second burst of air through the straw, try breathing in air, by sniffing through your nose. The intake of air must happen *during* the bubble-blowing with your cheeks. Don't go on until you have practised this and can do it *easily*.

Now two more steps: whilst blowing air with your cheeks, towards the end of your cheek air supply, relax your throat and continue to blow air using your lungs. *But*: try to keep your cheeks puffed out at the same time. Now try changing from cheek-puffing to lung-puffing so that *there is a continuous bubbling in the glass*. The final step is to take air in your lungs (through the nose) and change over to lung-blowing. When the lung supply is nearly gone, change to cheek-blowing and take more air through the nose to refill the lungs. It's all easy, except for the change over from cheeks to lungs, when there is often a small gap. Try to iron this out. Keep practising for some days until you can continue bubbling for a few minutes continuously whilst reading a book!

That stage should present no real difficulty. The hard part is to come, and if you are seriously bent on perfecting this technique on the flute you must be prepared for lots of_____ _____ and heaps of_____ _____! You will also need an inexhaustible supply of humour. Take the head-joint and try blowing, using your cheeks only. This can be very frustrating as when you do eventually get a sound, it's barely a tiny squeak. Persevere. It may work better if you block up the end of the tube with the palm of your hand, making it airtight. You may also have to change the way you blow (your embouchure) quite considerably to effect a rather weak sound. It will get better in time, though it usually takes many weeks, if not months, to get a sustained tone for more than a couple of seconds.

The next stage is to re-assemble your flute and try out a left-hand note. This is harder still. Now you must practise this for a few minutes several times a day. You will have to grow accustomed to using the muscles of the embouchure in a new way. You will need a lot of patience and a sense of humour. The change-over from cheeks to lungs and vice-versa is usually the hardest part. Don't worry if the sound stops; it won't eventually. This exercise below will help. Practise it rhythmically.

Now try changing notes during a breathing change-over.

The principle to guide you from here on must be to use circular breathing either during a trill or during a relatively easy note. Find the register which works best for you. Each person has individual difficulties and different embouchures, so there are no clear rules.

Is circular breathing really necessary? Some of today's music demands circular, or continuous, breathing. One performer has performed a piece lasting two hours and twenty-five minutes of continuous blowing! What about Bach? His music often requires organ-like long phrases. On the other hand, music, like speech, needs to breathe. It's a contradiction, rather like national politics. You alone can decide where, and how, if at all, to use it. There is a slight change of sound when the change-over takes place, but this can be skilfully overcome. You may think this technique crazy: learn to do it first, and laugh afterwards.

INTONATION
EXPRESSIVE INTONATION

Assuming that Practice Book 4 — Intonation and Vibrato – has been carefully read, the next stage is to play a few melodies, such as:
a) the opening Andante of the Bach C Major Sonata
b) the Adagio of the G minor Flute Concerto by Bach
c) The Swan, Saint-Saens
d) Concertino, Chaminade (slow sections and Cadenza)
e) Cantabile e Presto, Enesco, first page
f) Nocturne and Allegro Scherzando, Gaubert, first page
g) F Major Sonata (Larghetto), Handel
h) Sicilienne, Fauré

These, and many more, should be looked at in a new way.

Often, changing the pitch of a note in a phrase can make that phrase *more expressive*. Don't be stuck by rules; just use your instinct, or, in other words, your expressive 'ear'.

That statement sounds like a contradiction to Practice Book 4; it isn't. It is necessary to fully understand that Book before experimenting. You will find that when a decision has been made to flatten, or sharpen, a particular note in a phrase, the justification for doing so will probably be found in the chart on page 9 in Practice Book 4.

Experiment with these tunes, moving notes where they seem to want to go. In this way you will develop an expressive intonation.

Printed in Great Britain by Printwise (Haverhill) Limited, Suffolk 8/02 (44938)

TREVOR WYE

VIDEO

PLAY THE FLUTE
A beginner's guide

TUTORS

A BEGINNER'S BOOK FOR THE FLUTE
Part 1 (Practice Cassette available separately)
Part 2
Piano Accompaniment

FLUTE CLASS
A group teaching book for students and teachers

PRACTICE BOOKS FOR THE FLUTE
VOLUME 1 Tone (plus TONE CASSETTE available separately)
VOLUME 2 Technique
VOLUME 3 Articulation
VOLUME 4 Intonation and Vibrato
VOLUME 5 Breathing and Scales

A PICCOLO PRACTICE BOOK

PROPER FLUTE PLAYING

SOLO FLUTE

MUSIC FOR SOLO FLUTE

FLUTE & PIANO

A COUPERIN ALBUM
AN ELGAR FLUTE ALBUM
A FAURE FLUTE ALBUM
A RAMEAU ALBUM
A RAVEL ALBUM
A SATIE FLUTE ALBUM
A SCHUMANN FLUTE ALBUM
A VIVALDI ALBUM

A VERY EASY BAROQUE ALBUM, Volume 1
A VERY EASY BAROQUE ALBUM, Volume 2
A VERY EASY CLASSICAL ALBUM
A VERY EASY ROMANTIC ALBUM
A VERY EASY 20TH CENTURY ALBUM

A FIRST LATIN-AMERICAN FLUTE ALBUM
A SECOND LATIN-AMERICAN FLUTE ALBUM

MOZART FLUTE CONCERTO IN G K.313
MOZART FLUTE CONCERTO IN D K.314 AND ANDANTE IN G K.315

SCHUBERT THEME AND VARIATIONS D 935 No. 3

FLUTE ENSEMBLE

THREE BRILLIANT SHOWPIECES